Th… being

'As our eve… more fragile and the world around us changes fast, each of us needs to become stronger and more resilient. We need the spiritual power that comes from within – from the eternal store of peace, love and happiness that lies within us all, waiting to be discovered.'

In this simple book, Anthony Strano shows you how to do just that, revealing practical ways to build eight powers that are the keys to well-being: *introspection, discernment, decision-making, courage, letting go, tolerance, adjustment* and *co-operation.* When you start to tap into these positive qualities and use them to inform your everyday life, you will become truly powerful, freed from negativity, past and present, and filled with peace, energy and love.

Anthony Strano was born in Australia to Italian parents and co-ordinates the Brahma Kumaris centres in Greece, Hungary and Turkey. For more than thirty years he has travelled internationally, conducting lectures, workshops and seminars, and is known for his eloquent speaking and writing and his unique approach based on the time-tested principles of Raja Yoga meditation. He is author of *Slaying the Three Dragons* and *Seeking Silence*, published by Sterling Ethos New York. For further reading and audio material from Anthony Strano visit www.bkpublications.com.

The Quest for Well-being

Using Your 8 Powers

Anthony Strano

BRAHMA KUMARIS

BKIS

Anthony Strano
The Quest for Well-being ~ Using Your 8 Powers

First published in 2013 by Brahma Kumaris Information Services Ltd,
in association with Brahma Kumaris World Spiritual University (UK)
Registered Charity No: 269971
Global Co-operation House, 65 Pound Lane, London NW10 2HH, UK
www.bkpublications.com
email: enquiries@bkpublications.com
www.brahmakumaris.org

Print ISBN 978-1-886872-62-2
Kindle 978-1-886872-66-0
EPub 978-1-886872-67-7

Illustrator: Lotta Arbman
Designed by Makar Publishing Production
Printed in India by Imprint Digital

Contents

Introducing your inner powers 7
Introspection 11
Discernment 19
Decision-making 27
Courage 35
Letting go 43
Tolerance 51
Adjustment 57
Co-operation 63

Introducing your inner powers

This is a time of great change – economically, politically, and socially. As the world becomes seemingly more fragile and our everyday lives splinter without warning, each of us – and our society in general – needs to become stronger, more powerful. But what does it mean to be powerful? Spiritually, we understand that power, or strength, has nothing to do with force or aggression. Spiritual power comes from within – from the eternal store of positive resources, such as peace, love and happiness, that lies within each of us, even if we are not yet aware of it.

Power has so many aspects, all intertwined like the threads in a tapestry. We cannot separate one from another because the tapestry as a whole depends on each thread being used in the right way, at the right place. So, although this book describes eight powers – introspection, discernment, decision-making, courage, letting go, tolerance, adjustment and co-operation – many more powers intertwine with them to bring about well-being. These eight powers must also interweave between themselves if they are to be effective.

When we start to tap into these positive qualities and use them to inform our everyday behaviour, we will become truly powerful. We will inhabit a state of consciousness in which we are not influenced by negativity in any form – we no longer experience feelings of selfishness or violence, dislike, anger, revenge or resentment. Freeing the mind and heart from negativity, brings peace. And peace leads to another quality so essential for these current times – stability. Stability helps us to maintain order and balance in life.

Spiritual powers – we might call them values or virtues – also bring about neutrality, the ability to find perspective and inclusiveness, moving beyond personal likes and dislikes when dealing with people.

The powers work particularly well when combined with virtues like simplicity and respect. Simplicity leads to economy, and spiritual economy helps us to respect our personal resources – of thought, word and time – as well as the resources of Mother Nature. When we become more economical by leading a more simple life, abundance follows: we tap into our natural capacity for selfless generosity and co-operation with others and, through this, experience well-being.

Respect works like spiritual alchemy, turning the worst situation into the best and making the impossible possible. Respect for all things means accepting differences. It is the basis of authentic love.

By learning to manage and balance all these innate powers, we uncover an ability to act appropriately, to be creative, to construct newness and hope and to achieve personal aims while creating a respectful place for other people, time and nature itself.

Cultivating these powers does not happen all at once; it requires attentiveness and time. We become more attentive by observing which power is required at a particular time, in a particular situation, or in a particular relationship. This keeps our behaviour and attitude positive, which is the first step towards experiencing true spiritual power.

By looking inside, you will observe obstacles to co-operation. When you make the decision to conquer them, you will notice that your mind feels peaceful. In this peace you can co-operate with anything or anyone – at any level – without fear or conflict. You are free.

Power 1

Introspection

In a world where everything has become showy, noisy and full of superficialities, it is difficult to appreciate the power of introspection. Though it is the greatest means to refresh ourselves, we sometimes forget to use the art of quietness, which simply means becoming still for a few moments. When we experiment by using a little introspective quietness, we quickly appreciate its ability to recharge and strengthen the inner life.

WHAT IS INTROSPECTION?

Introspection is about stepping inside and meeting 'myself' a few times during the day. It is not about rejecting life and its challenges, neither is it about isolation. We choose to be quiet and turn inwards not out of fear or distaste but because it fills us with confidence and a sense of direction. It provides an opportunity to reflect on and understand the patterns in the self that create problems and require change. It gives us the insight to begin changing ourselves.

Create a healthy distance from outside pressure and rush; a space away from the bombardment of opinions, words, deadlines, worries and fears.

MY AIM

To tune myself in so that I can live in a coherent and positive way. Through this I will be able to live in this world of entanglements more easily and when events slam into me without warning, I will feel more secure and grounded.

LOOKING WITHIN

By sampling inner silence, we meet the roots of our being – the soul-self – and discover the original energies of peace, love and happiness. This discovery is not just on an intellectual level; we actually 'feel' these energies as a personal reality. This is very empowering.

In this tranquil solitude we step away from the extroversion, clamour and rush of daily life and rest in a still point of quietness. In that stillness, there is always calm and relief from the burden of unnecessary thoughts, words and deeds. This inner quietness recharges our battery and refills our spiritual fuel tank. Only by becoming introspective can we connect with this original and eternal part of ourselves.

True introspection creates a position of neutrality – we step aside from unhelpful concepts and wrong conclusions about ourselves and others. Being in this neutral state for a while helps us to find answers to any questions. It brings peace and detachment from the emotional red tape that defines our relationships with ourselves and the world around us. It frees the mind and gives it the clarity to cut out the trivia and habitual clinging to unnecessary detail that blocks our perception of the bigger picture.

CONTEMPLATION

- I sit quietly and look within.
- I become so quiet, so quickly and so deeply.
- Whilst staying at the bottom of my inner ocean, the outside waves and even tsunamis of emotion cannot find me, let alone hit me.
- I feel at one with myself.
- Here I can decide whether to stay inside and stabilise myself in this peace, or examine the changes I need to make to improve the situation.
- I discern clearly what is best to think, say or do.
- I am not pushed by fear of others' expectations or demands.
- I feel safe.
- I can decide when and how to act.

SOME GUIDELINES

Once inside, with the real self, watch and evaluate any thoughts, feelings and responses, and examine whether they are appropriate.

Ask the following questions:

1. Do I have any habits that have a negative impact on my daily interactions?
2. How have these habits embedded themselves in me and become part of my personality?
3. How can I start to shift, or dissolve, these bad habits?

DUAL CONNECTION

When we look inside, we can also tune into God, the reservoir of unconditional power that recharges us. From this quiet point, we do not just remain in a state of observation, we are re-energised and pulled back into expression with the strength and willingness to fully participate in life outside.

By going deeper inside and concentrating completely on the original self, we draw closer to the Supreme Source and receive a current of pure energy that dissolves bad habits. For this energy to be truly transformative, we must realise the importance of exercising introspective concentration often. Practising regularly, for a few seconds every hour, helps to conquer the tyranny of bad habits.

QUESTIONS TO ASK

In the silence of introspection the self awakens and can hear us. Ask it the three questions below. The answers may come as you sit in introspective silence, or later in the day, perhaps as sudden realisations or signals from others.

1. What is my hope for myself?
2. What is God's hope for me?
3. What is life calling me to do?

GETTING IT RIGHT

The sign of true introspection is happiness and optimism. If, after going inside, you feel quiet but gloomy or not like communicating, you may have misunderstood the practice. Rather than connecting to the rejuvenating current, you have become disconnected. A faulty socket can plug us into irritation, dislike and self-centredness, causing us perhaps to see the weakness of others or lament the past.

In order to repair the fault, become aware of any repeating patterns of negative thoughts, feelings or words, either by observing the self, listening to others' remarks or noticing repetitive painful situations. As far as possible, try to pinpoint and understand the habits and mechanisms that dominate this attitude and vision and decide to move away from such patterns.

Choose a more appropriate socket – become more detached or optimistic, or simply put a stop to the traffic of the mind and heart by telling them to be quiet, to be still and to remain in peace. The clarity brought about by such introspection gets us back on track and keeps everything moving forwards.

Some bad habits are like tyrants – they crowd the head and heart so strongly that under no circumstances do they wish to move. They have enjoyed their undisputed reign over us and will not depart easily. To defeat them, it's important to keep practising and to connect with the Eternal Reservoir of benevolent energy.

Sometimes these subtle, clever tyrants try to deceive us or break our resolve. So, in order to achieve complete mastery, we need to learn how to step back from a situation and see more clearly.

That is the second power we need to develop – the power of discernment.

Power 2

Discernment

Discernment takes place in the reflective state of introspection. In this state we see ourselves and the world as they truly are – and this equips us to make the best and most beneficial decisions for ourselves and those with whom we interact. Without proper discernment, we are in danger of repeating mistakes and returning to old problems; we remain unable to see the reality of a situation and create viable solutions to its challenges and responses to its opportunities.

WHAT IS DISCERNMENT?

True discernment is the ability to step back from ourselves, a situation and the influence of others, see a clear picture and then choose how to act for the best. To discern does not mean to pass judgment and neatly compartmentalise something or someone – to stick on a convenient label and

The power of discernment is the greatest of all keys.

then feel secure because things have been put in order. To take this approach is to rely on ingrained habits – and effective discernment is never hijacked by such things. If we are to discern accurately, we need first to reach a state of peace and be able to keep the self neutral. Otherwise, the quality of our discernment will be damaged by habitual emotions and reactions.

MY AIM

To recognise and overcome any negativity or problem in a wise and firm way.

WHY NOW?

In order to remain emotionally and mentally healthy, we must be able to see through illusion. The power of discernment protects us from getting entangled in the illusions generated not only by ourselves but also by the society in which we live.

Discernment is especially welcome now because it is so easy to be deceived in today's world, with its glamorous presentation of materialistic values. It is seen as good and normal to value goods and own things; this is regarded as security.

But time shows that security cannot come from such values, but only from honest intentions and respectful actions.

Desire and fear can cajole us into accepting such values and lifestyles as good and necessary, even though they can never lead to real happiness. The lifestyle may initially seem satisfying, but ultimately such illusions destroy true contentment. It is hard to break away from this way of thinking. The habitual patterns of desire and fear that lie behind it reign in us for years and we become addicted to their power, however painful that may be. Discernment protects us from the influence of such tyrants.

THE ESSENCE

Silence increases the quality and the level of our ability to discern, allowing us to use our time, thoughts and qualities effectively and thus benefit all. In the silence of inner quietness, the intellect makes everything clear and then we just know how to act for the best. Too much analysis and mental processing pollutes the clarity of discernment; an overload of details makes us miss the essence.

CONTEMPLATION

- I sit quietly and look within.
- In the silence of introspection I become like a child again.
- I am open and trust life.
- I move away from any arrogant attachment to knowing and doing.
- I humbly open myself to relearning.
- I see life in a new way.
- I learn from all experiences without exception.

PRIORITISING

What do we need to discern above all else? Ourselves. In reality, deception comes from within since we only see what we want to believe. If we cannot discern the way in which we affect others, then our relationships cannot improve. If we cannot discern how our misunderstandings and habitual ways of behaving cloud the mind then, instead of discerning, we will fall back into the trap of discriminating and judging.

Often, we do not 'see' the self and, as a result, perpetuate cycles of conflict, animosity and unhappiness in ourselves and those around us. What we cannot see, we cannot change, so things get worse. Enlightenment, or the 'click' of something turning on, is the seeing or discernment of reality. With this shift of consciousness, sometimes referred to as the 'opening of the third (spiritual) eye', comes a great release from the fear, doubt and fluctuation in thought that can cripple lives.

SOME GUIDELINES

One major benefit of discernment is that it reveals the source of our inner strength. To be strong, or powerful, means that we do not have to resort to anger, comparisons, labelling and threats in the face of opposition or a difficult situation. Instead, we discern which spiritual medicine to use – kindness, accommodation, detachment – and this heals us and the lives of those with whom we are connected. To be powerful, it's important to repeat the following affirmations regularly:

1. 'I remember my original self' – the spiritual self holds the resources for healing.
2. 'I act with consideration' – and allow this to replace manipulative, selfish interactions.
3. 'I connect with the Divine Source' – this offers unlimited co-operation as we create our own well-being.

BEING HUMBLE

The power of discernment only develops accurately and effectively if we are humble. The openness that comes from humility is accompanied by a respect for ourselves, other people and new situations. It brings a fresh perspective and new understanding. Discernment, polished by humility, protects both the self and the integrity of a task.

THE PITFALLS

If the power of discernment starts out crooked, it can descend into cruel discrimination and merciless judgment. Then we play the judge and encase others in neat boxes with convenient labels and consequently no longer think about, or review, our opinions. Or we may play the 'saviour' and interfere with someone, rather than just support him or her. This can lead to mutual dependency and a loss in freedom for both of us.

When the power of discernment is working accurately, we become able to discern the point at which we are responsible and where other people are responsible for themselves – and are able to use mercy and compassion to help remove sorrow without getting entangled in it.

GETTING IT RIGHT

To increase the power of discernment, it's important to practise introspection and silence every day and have the humility to look at things from different perspectives and constantly relearn. We should never take for granted the things we have already learned.

Accurate discerning can take a single moment, or it might take a day or longer, depending on what there is to understand. You may need more time to work out an appropriate response if a situation or experience is new, or if you catch yourself falling into negative habitual ways of behaving or reacting to people and events. It takes time to discern why we allow this.

It's important to remember, too, that it is not enough simply to discern – we must also make a decision and act on it. If we do not do this, the power of discernment will remain an observation, and even if that observation is accurate, it will never become a personal reality. We do not gain power from a decision until we have acted on it.

This brings us to the third power – the power of decision-making.

Power 3

Decision-making

If, after employing the power of discernment, we do not decide and not act, we are left only with theories and opinions. These do not empower us but, instead, leave us stuck in a cycle of living that we wish to break out of but cannot. This leads to frustration because we can see what is happening, but lack the strength to change it. We can feel helpless; a puppet in life rather than a master of it. So, although discernment is a major key in accessing well-being, we cannot turn that key until we develop the power of making determined decisions. And to be really effective, we need to act as soon as we have discerned what needs to be done.

WHAT IS DECISION-MAKING?

Decision-making involves never being afraid to take responsibility for making a decision. It is said, 'he who hesitates is lost'. When we have doubts we lack the courage to decide and act. This indicates a lack of perception, will and, possibly, an underlying resistance to change. We might have the tendency to complain rather than change. Remaining stagnant in this way can also indicate a lack of self-respect. Self-respect is one of the deepest motivators in effective decision-making.

MY AIM

I will have respect for myself. Once I am sure of something and its necessity in my life, I will have the courage to act and make that something a living reality in myself. I will not worry about theoretical knowledge – about values, ethics and codes of behaviour – this can become a burden and make the soul weaker.

TAKING THE PLUNGE

To develop successful decision-making, we need to be willing to take responsibility for our choices, no matter what they bring about. We need to be fearless and adventurous – 'nothing ventured nothing gained' goes the saying. When the will is not strong enough, it is hard to make a decision. When inner ambivalence is a result of a lack of commitment

Never put off for tomorrow what can be done today.

to change, or a lack of a sense of responsibility towards ourselves, fluctuation can follow. We might wish to change to something better but also want to stay as we are, which though uncomfortable is at least safe. Such fluctuation can become another habit that prevents us from focusing our willpower and being decisive.

CONTEMPLATION

- I sit quietly and look within.
- I go beyond excuses, and beyond fear of what others might think, say or do.
- I stay on track. Although there are many distractions on the road, with determination, commitment and focus I empower myself and translate decisions into effective actions.

THE ROOTS OF DETERMINATION

Where does determination come from? From having faith in our decisions; being able to say, 'I have chosen this decision because at this moment it is the right thing to do, it is necessary'.

A particular decision comes from a particular aim. Having faith in that aim creates a determined thought – that no matter what, I must do what I have set out to do. At the same time, we need to remain flexible enough to meet circumstances as they arise, but not to compromise what we have committed to do.

If we choose not to make decisions about life and, instead, allow others to take action for us, animosity and resentment will build up. We will feel like a puppet, a victim and a plaything of the cosmos, exploited or hard done-by. When we realise that such reactions are just excuses or complaints made to justify a current situation, honesty will inspire us to decide to change everything. We will no longer linger in self-pity or self-doubt but, instead, will change the thoughts that create our inner world.

SOME GUIDELINES

Having decided to change the quality of your life – because if you don't, who will? – it's important to keep the following thoughts in mind; you might repeat them to yourself as affirmations at points throughout the day:

1. 'My decisions, or lack of decisions, determine the reality of my life' – if we do not take responsibility for how we live, life will feel unfair and oppressive. Making a decision not to live like this anymore is to realise that, at last, we can choose our life's direction – and this brings a feeling of empowerment.
2. 'Create rather than wait' – at least not for too long! Seeing the options, choose what to do now rather than wait for the ideal time, person or circumstance to arrive

before acting decisively. Though patience is important, it's important not to become passive.

3. Ask, 'Why am I deciding, or not deciding, on something?' – being clear about and fully conscious of a stance spares future regret.

DECISIONS AND OTHERS

It is one thing to make a decision affecting our own lives, but quite another to make decisions that affect the lives of others. This concern is particularly relevant for people in positions of authority – for parents, teachers, ministers, doctors, lawyers – who have to make decisions carefully, responsibly and wisely, taking into account the needs, aims, aspirations and personality of others.

Decisions that affect another person, a shared task or a relationship must involve mutual decision-making and agreement. Dictatorial decisions show a lack of discernment and respect. Over time, such decision-making leads to crisis – not just personally, but in the environment, the economy and society. Selfish concerns are felt by others taking part in the decision-making process, and as a result, people do not put their heart into a task or relationship. Although superficially acquiesce, in some subtle way they will refuse to co-operate because they feel the deception. Without personal, internal and heartfelt co-operation, a task or relationship never gains momentum.

GETTING IT RIGHT

Lack of commitment, dependence on others for encouragement, being influenced by others' opinions – all block the power of decision-making. Sometimes we constantly ask others for advice, secretly hoping that they will make a decision on our behalf. Then if something goes wrong we conveniently have someone to blame. Before asking for (or giving) advice, we need to discern our motives.

If after making a decision and acting on it, the result is not what was expected, don't worry but just try again. The very fact that you made the decision and acted on it shows that a shift has taken place within (even if it was not visible). Then discern how to do better next time. No sincere action is ever wasted – it breaks the ground of old habits and starts to challenge the tyrants that have governed past actions. Seeds have been planted; now wait patiently to see the flower and fruit. Honest motives and determined decisions create an inner trust that success will come; the rest is simply a matter of time.

Decisions – whether about ourselves or others – require transparency of purpose. We must understand why we have chosen to act in a certain way and not in another way. Without such honesty, trust is lost. Discerning, making a decision and acting are natural partners – we need to put all three into practice to progress and attain understanding and well-being.

To clearly decide and do, requires not only a sense of responsibility and clarity, but also courage. Hesitation, passivity and doubt camouflage fear and tend to linger in the mind even after we have made a clear decision. Courage is the strongest antidote available.

This is the fourth power we have to develop – the power of courage.

Power 4

Courage

Although the power of accurate decision-making comes from discernment, the determination to put it into practice comes from courage. Without courage we become a victim to fears, excuses and hesitancy. Courage creates the enthusiasm to persevere and the ability to see things positively – when we do this, problems never turn into barriers.

WHAT IS COURAGE?

Courage is the ability to pursue aims no matter what. The essence of courage is faith: faith in our aims and a deep understanding of why we have chosen a particular course of action. Determination, patience, enthusiasm and good company sustain courage. Once the goal has been set, reaching it becomes a matter of self-respect. We cannot just give up or give in to negativity, no matter from where or whom it comes.

Patience keeps the self peaceful and enables the self to co-operate, adjust to unexpected events and overcome barriers in a non-violent way. Without it we might become over-focused or try too intensely to achieve a goal.

Enthusiasm is an energy that raises perception to such an extent that anything feels possible. This is how miracles happen.

Good company also sustains courage. We all enjoy being with people who share in and work for the same ideals, commit themselves to a shared vision or goal and support each other's efforts through thick and thin.

MY AIM

I will develop the courage to face my illusions. I need courage to do this because I have believed they are real for so long.

DIVINE COMPANIONSHIP

In the Indian scripture the Bhagavad Gita, the great warrior Arjuna is able to emerge out of his doubts and fears and have courage because of his companionship with his divine friend. Very often in history and storytelling we see how a

If I take one step of courage, then God takes a thousand steps towards me.

a good companion enables his or her friend to achieve the best and rise above obstacles – they call on their courage to keep going no matter what. Such friendship empowers the other and reminds him or her of their task, capacities and destiny. Many of the heroes and heroines in mythology across the world are assisted by a particular god or goddess – and always because of the innate worth of those heroes.

Various spiritual paths affirm that God, as guide and friend, is the true support and companion of the human soul as it strives to conquer the dark tyrants within. The divine love coming from this Benevolent Friend supplies the constant light of courage and determination. Such companionship with God and like-minded human friends certainly helps to overcome the dragons of fear, doubt, worry, remorse, guilt and ego.

The soul must become a spiritual warrior who, with the sword of wisdom, dissolves obstacles into nothingness whatever tyrant or dragon tries to defeat it, saying, 'As a warrior, I expose all my foes as illusions'.

SOME GUIDELINES

The many small and big obstacles that appear daily and unexpectedly can become stepping-stones, rather than insurmountable mountains, if the following thoughts are adhered to. Keep them in mind through the day:

1. 'Trust in my aim and decision creates the courage to make the impossible possible' – losing even a small amount of trust or faith creates a 'delete button' in the consciousness. So we must affirm daily, 'I keep trust and keep faith in who I am and where I am going'.
2. 'Words like "if", "because", "perhaps", "tomorrow" and "I don't know" dissolve courage' – excuses pollute the will, then it becomes easy to slip back into a state of doubt. Our vocabulary reflects our inner state, so observe it carefully and choose determined, positive thoughts and words to sustain courage and will.
3. 'I will regularly renew my aim and direction' – never carry yesterday's events into today; instead say, 'I am a student of the past rather than its slave'. This attitude of learning carries us forward and creates natural courage.

HEROIC BEHAVIOUR

The main quality of a hero is courage – not a reckless bravado, full of impulse and ambition, but a quiet, introspective courage. In that quietness, the hero is able to discern and then decide on a particular course of action. He might see that it is better to let go of another person's past rather than hold it against them or constantly remind them of it. With humility and courage the past is forgiven; the hero completely lets go. Only heroes can do such things.

Heroes reflect deeply and silently before they speak and act. They have the courage to observe themselves and see what internal changes are necessary to improve their quality of interaction. Besides courage, heroes also require authenticity of character and nobility of spirit if they are to attain a high ideal. Attainment of such ideals will not just happen or comprise a few momentary conquests. This is a life-long quest.

The quest for inner excellence – liberation from negative forces – has always been the goal of all heroes, whether in myth or real life. Today, as ever, the greatest courage is to discern and decide to eliminate the darkness that comes in myriad forms from our own characters. For example, we might discern that an attachment to someone is limiting them and decide to let go of that selfishness rather than hold on to and justify it. This requires compassionate courage and the armour of honesty.

CONTEMPLATION

- I sit quietly and look within with honesty.
- Honesty enables me to be clear about my motives, to discern the subtle mechanisms of selfishness that sap my courage and transform my motives.
- Through deep honesty with myself and the Divine, I have no fear when facing anything negative, unexpected or difficult.
- The burdens of life become light; I feel relieved, peaceful and content.

GETTING IT RIGHT

It takes honesty as well as courage to give ourselves a good shake and see things for what they are, not what we imagine them to be. To see is far better than not to see. Without honest vision we will keep being deceived by illusion and trapped by sorrow and game-playing. It is time to set ourselves free – it just takes a little courage and some letting go.

This is the fifth power we need – the power to let go.

Power 5

Letting go

It takes courage to let go and return to our essence – but it is only in this essence that we find truth and freedom. To let go of habitual attractions and the thrill of indulging in dramatic behaviour and finally to get to the point requires a firm decision – and the courage to take that decision to heart.

WHAT IS LETTING GO?

Letting go is all about realising that nothing and no one can disturb our peace of mind except ourselves. The thought that other people and external situations are doing things to us causes much unhappiness. Maybe they are doing things, but we need to let go of being so influenced by them. It takes courage and determination to let go of justifying anger, of defending ourselves in order to blame others, of wasteful thoughts and feelings that have become ingrained habits. It takes courage to realise and then act in the awareness that we create well-being in our lives irrespective of the things around us.

MY AIM

Rather than thinking about what I should or could have done or been, I must let go of guilt and blame, discern what has to change inside and decide to do it no matter what.

ACT OF LIBERATION

The mind has a mind of its own. Stimulated by bad feelings or negative emotions, thoughts expand, race and tumble around our heads at colossal speed. The result is tension, stress and tiredness. It is a great liberation to be able to let go rather than allowing these thoughts and emotions such free-reign. It is simple, too: in the second we notice ourselves heightening any thought or feeling, we just ask the mind to put on the brake before the emotional or verbal head-on collision.

To let go means putting a full stop to all this mental activity with one simple thought: 'I am a being of peace'. Thought creates consciousness, so if we repeat this phrase slowly and attentively, our thoughts and emotions stop expanding and

In letting go of superficial identities, I remember who I really am: a spiritual being.

inner peace is restored. The essence of our being is peace – complete freedom from overload. To return to this essential peace means observing the mind's antics and deciding to put a full stop on them now; no lingering. Of course, the mind does not listen at first. We have to gently and firmly repeat the direction 'stop'. If we do not, those wasteful thoughts will crush us once again.

SOME GUIDELINES

To help let go of illusions and superficialities and return to the essence of the self and of life, repeat these reminder affirmations quietly during the day, anywhere and anytime:

1. 'I have the courage to be myself' – this means remembering 'who I am' and letting go of any masks and other defences now.
2. 'I see the essence of others. They, too, are eternal points of being' – within every costume is an actor. This affirmation is all about seeing that valuable point of being and let go of any prejudices about colour, gender, nationality, the past and any weaknesses. It's important to appreciate the specialty of everyone. Seeing in this way takes courage.

3. 'I let go of the words "I" and "my"' – these concepts are the cause of all conflicts in the world.
4. 'I remember the Divine' – and in return receive the unconditional current of love that helps us to let go of any and every malice.

LETTING GO OF DESIRE

We must understand that we are all souls, a point of consciousness and the essence of life. The soul has a mind, an intellect and patterns of thinking. Some of these patterns are original and pure; others are polluted and negative. The latter create selfish desires and needs that demand to be fulfilled. But even when they are fulfilled, the sense of contentment does not last long; instead it stimulates even stronger desires for more money, or a bigger house and so on. Such desires can kick-start processes of manipulation, control and of sabotaging others who get in our way.

This type of thinking and living creates an inner bomb that eventually explodes, which is why so many people find themselves feeling lonely, stressed, depressed, disoriented, empty and angry. Letting go of such dysfunctional desires and aims and returning to the essence of ourselves heals these negative emotions.

How do we let go and return to this essence? By practising meditation. In meditation we learn that one 'essenceful' thought concentrated upon in silence recharges the self. Such a thought, when repeated slowly a few times in a state of introspective silence, recharges the self and then the self automatically lets go of stress, worry and anger.

CONTEMPLATION

- I sit quietly and look within.
- I concentrate on the thought, 'I am a spiritual being, my essence is peace.'
- I repeat slowly to myself a few times, 'I am a soul'.
- Peace is my essence, peace is my freedom.
- I am peace.

RETURN TO THE SOURCE

The essence of a tree after it has let go of its leaves, flowers, branches, trunk and roots is the seed. Similarly, the essence of consciousness is a thought, the essence of time a second, the essence of love respect, the essence of happiness contentment, and the essence of abundance simplicity. Many essences form the foundation of power, but, above all, it is the essence of one pure positive thought in one second that helps us quickly to empower the self.

In certain situations we are forced immediately to let go and arrive at the point of what is to be thought or done. When firemen are called to a raging fire, they have to let go of questions such as how hot the fire is, who started it and the cost of the damage and immediately act to put out the fire. Later they look into the questions but, while the fire rages, the urgent need is to put it out in the quickest and most effective way.

The same underlying principle applies to our search for well-being. We need to return to life's basics and let go of complicated formulas, especially when the temptation comes to wallow in negative emotions, or use intellectual cleverness to threaten our happiness. Well-being comes with awareness and practice, and from prioritising peace and stability.

GETTING IT RIGHT

Negative thoughts and feelings seem to expand like balloons – it's hard to let go of them. In comparison, positive thoughts and feelings are slower, deeper, lighter and fewer. Unlike their negative counterparts, positive thoughts immediately translate into action. The self, having let go of endless rounds of thinking and discussing clever theories and opinions, just acts.

We have so many ideas, plans and opinions. They may be well expressed and well intentioned, but rarely do we put them into action; they are not sustained because often we lack the power to translate them into reality in our personal life. Why? Because other people's criticism, defamation and non-co-operation, or our own lack of coherence or lack of courage deflates those balloons.

Only by letting go of the great expansion of our social and physical identity and returning to the essence of our being – the soul-self – will we find unlimited peace. In this letting go of superficial identities we remember who we really are: a spiritual being. When we let go of divisive self-positioning and of jumping to superficial conclusions about people and situations, and when we embrace difference as the wonder of life, then we start to truly respect ourselves and others.

This is the sixth power we need to cultivate – the power of tolerance.

Power 6

Tolerance

Tolerance is a positive energy that comes primarily from knowing our purpose in life and being content and fulfilled by it. Then we welcome difference rather than being annoyed or frightened by it. As with all the powers, everything comes back to where we are with ourselves. When we have a good relationship with ourselves and it is working well, we have the power to be open and inclusive. When it is not so good, fear may cause us to reject and become intolerant of others.

WHAT IS TOLERANCE?

True tolerance is about respecting and accepting difference. It means giving up any expectation that people and situations will be the way we want them to be. It requires the realisation that we do not need to control people and circumstances to make things go right – and that time, intention and other factors play their part in life. When we understand this, we can be truly tolerant.

MY AIM

To reach the state where I can be neutral and just allow things to be, whether they suit me or not. All things have their right to exist and express themselves. When I am rooted in my original state of self-awareness, when I know my part within this unlimited play of life and get on with it, then I can make space for others to play their part too.

OVERCOMING DIFFICULTIES

Many people have a faulty understanding of the power of tolerance. Some see it as a patronising attitude, in which one person puts his or herself in a superior position to another person or situation. Tolerance cannot flourish in superiority-inferiority situations. Arrogance makes one person think that they are better than another person – believing that they know the right way, they may tolerate the other person rather than openly come into conflict.

A submissive position is also unhelpful. Some people tend to tolerate the anger or bad behaviour of others and keep

Accepting that we all belong creates a generous heart which includes others, no matter how different they are.

quiet, swallowing every reaction until the stomach is filled with resentful tension. This might be called tolerance, but in fact it shows that fear and lack of self-respect are blocking assertiveness. If we wish to please at all costs, if we want approval and fear rejection, we will lack the courage to communicate clearly and assertively. We must wake up, take stock of ourselves and realise that neither exploding in anger nor swallowing reactions provide a solution. Some real solutions are to be found in the following thoughts.

SOME GUIDELINES

It's important that we write the script of our lives in such a way that we feel fulfilled and others are happy and appreciative. To do this, try saying these affirmations every day:

1. 'I am aware of my role in life' – we must seek to understand our own scripts and why we have been allocated certain roles.
2. 'I avoid becoming entangled in the roles of others' – this is as important as avoiding entanglement in our own self-centred desires and opinions.
3. 'I share what I am selflessly' – when we share without attaching strings, we grow and are appreciated in the hearts of others without having to ask, hope for or expect appreciation. In this pure, selfless state, we remain free of expectations of other people, who naturally and generously share what they are with us.

WORKING WITH OTHERS

Tolerance is about creating a space for quality interaction with others. Quality is the result of equality. We need to understand that all beings have innate good qualities and that each of us has an eternal part inside which we must express in our own unique way. When we develop this equality of vision, we will respect, accept and appreciate the existence of others. This uncluttered coming together, each with the other, complements difference. For each one, being unique offers something different but necessary to the whole. This is how the play of life is meant to be.

CONTEMPLATION

- I sit quietly and look within.
- I accept that we are all actors on the world stage.
- Each of us has a unique and valuable expression that contributes to the wonderful variety of people and cultures on the earth.
- The Eternal Director of the great play allows us to write our own scripts.
- I am only able to interact happily with others when I accept their scripts, too.
- Then I avoid conflicts based on who is best or worst, right or wrong, superior or inferior, first or last – all of which define the times we live in.
- Genuine tolerance expresses itself in equality, generosity and inclusiveness – this is the natural condition of life.

GETTING IT RIGHT

Tolerance is a great power when understood correctly, but when misunderstanding muddles it, it can become a burden not only to us but also to the ones on the receiving end of any so-called 'tolerance'. By following the guidelines above, we will no longer need the word 'tolerance' in our vocabulary.

We can simply stop thinking about it! But until we reach this state of consciousness, we need to keep applying the principles and using the word. When we respect difference, we become naturally inclusive and tune into others.

This is the way to develop the seventh power – the power of adjustment.

Power 7

Adjustment

True tolerance makes us flexible. And when we are flexible we can accommodate and adjust to anything and anyone and maintain well-being. The ability to bend without breaking is linked to the amount of tolerance we develop. When we are fully flexible, we become able to adjust to the most unexpected, negative and difficult situations and people.

WHAT IS ADJUSTMENT?

To adjust or accommodate means to let go of past wounds, dislikes and prejudices until they dissolve completely, until not a trace is left. Often we may outwardly adjust, but inwardly we store up hurt and wrongs, real or imagined. This internal store poisons any chance we have of reconciliation or of mending past grievances. If we let go of this and reconnect to the inner essentials – the peace, love and purity we are born with – we will be able to adjust to any eventuality, heal the most diseased relationships and bring together the most disparate people.

MY AIM

I will connect to my roots – the blueprint of the original soul, which is made up of peace, love and purity – and experience them as a personal reality. From such a sound inner position I can adjust to any external situation and become extremely flexible without compromising myself.

STARTING POINT

We only develop the flexibility we need to cultivate the power of adjustment if, like a tree, we set down firm inner roots to keep us stable. A tree's capacity to bend depends on the depth of its roots. If they are too shallow, a storm will easily topple the tree. If our own inner roots are not linked to our eternal self, or original blueprint, then the power of flexibility will degenerate and a state of compromise will ensue.

If we compromise deeply held values and principles, either through fear or lack of awareness, we lose in the game of

life. We cannot be victorious; others who have maintained their integrity win, but we cannot because the self has been compromised. When we stop being true to ourselves we lose the power to win. And without claiming victory over negativity, difficulties and bad feelings, the self falls into a state of despair or frustrated anger.

CONTEMPLATION

- I sit quietly and look within.
- Tapping down into my inner roots – my soul energy – I dissolve the hurt, resentment and bad feelings that have accumulated within me.
- This dissolving makes me feel light.
- It frees me from the burden of anger and feelings of injustice.
- In this lightness I have the clarity to find alternatives.
- I stop measuring mistakes and the wrongs of others and myself.
- I create a different way of seeing and relating to life.

RECONCILIATION

In a world of bad feelings and long-standing resentment on personal, societal, national and global levels, the ability to accommodate to the existence of others is an urgent necessity. To adjust through reconciliation means stepping into other people's shoes and resting there for a while. It involves empathising with another way of perceiving the world, another way of evaluating and relating to life, rather than always making our own view the reference point.

In order to accommodate all differences, we must first reach a state of neutrality and inner peace. This is the basis of reconciliation. From this position we become able to build a bridge to understanding, letting go and forgiving, appreciating everything.

SOME GUIDELINES

To enhance the communication and empathy so necessary for unity and avoid the all-too common sense of isolation, repeat the following affirmations through the day, which offer bridge-building strategies:

1. 'I maintain a desire for oneness, harmony and balance' – let this thought inform everything, from ideals to practical necessities.
2. 'I keep connected to my original roots' – this helps to overcome the ego and attachments that splinter the whole.
3. 'I will tread gently' – this opens the way to reconciliation.

GETTING IT RIGHT

Be aware that the degree to which people are disunited governs the extent of their fragility. As things – relationships, tasks, goals – become more fragile, they are more likely to break into pieces, making it extra important that we follow the third guideline above, and tread gently in our relationships with others.

To effectively build the power of adjustment and fit in, we need to keep feeling light and peaceful and to appreciate the interplay of others in the fulfilment of our daily tasks.

This is the eighth power we need to develop – the power of co-operation.

Power 8

Co-operation

Natural co-operation is one of the most obvious characteristics of nature – without it nothing can fully function. The left brain co-operates with the right brain, one eye co-operates with the other, the heart and blood co-operate – and if this does not happen, disease follows. Disease throws everything off balance so that it becomes a struggle for the body to function, or even to survive. A similar lack of co-operation in any system leads to dysfunctional characteristics.

What causes a lack of co-operation? In brief, a deep attachment to the self – to our own ways of thinking and our own fears and prejudices. Such selfish feelings and attitudes cause us to become caged in our tiny self so that all experiences are filtered through that.

WHAT IS CO-OPERATION?

Co-operation is the interplay of tolerance, accommodation, flexibility, respect and appreciation of difference and uniqueness. When based on this interplay, co-operation is at the heart of any successful task.

No matter how capable, talented, efficient or extraordinary an individual may be, without co-operation from others, no single person can develop their personal skills. Neither can we implement a task without the assistance of a parent, teacher or mentor.

For example, an actor or singer needs musicians, producers, directors and especially an audience in order to express themselves successfully, despite their innate capacity for creativity and entertaining others.

Being able to appreciate the contribution of others and being open to that influence always facilitates the fulfillment of a task or a talent. It is said that even God – as powerful as God is – cannot accomplish a divine task without the assistance of His angels.

Unity, oneness harmony is that state of being where natural co-operation occurs.

Co-operation becomes natural and flows easily when we position ourselves confidently and humbly, leaving a space where others can enter and co-create with us.

MY AIM

I will strive, over time, to cultivate co-operation in my life – so that all those I come into contact with are content and can use their specialties wholeheartedly. I can do this by building respectful relationships.

BUILDING LONG-LASTING CO-OPERATION

The power of co-operation is natural – on this planet nothing could exist without it. How could we human beings thrive without the co-operation of the trees, plants, air, earth and sunlight? Within nature's kingdom we see many examples of mutually beneficial co-operation. We ourselves live in a society that could not exist if there was no co-operation. We go to the doctor for health matters, to the baker for bread, to the lawyer for legal advice, to the grocer for supplies. Even if society is not working as well as it could, still each of us is providing a much needed service for others.

Co-operation starts with the inner co-operation, or coherence, of thoughts, feelings and attitudes. Then co-operation with the world outside is easy. People are open and accepting if they feel that they can trust us. If our internal and external worlds do not co-operate harmoniously, we will exist in a state of disorientation and strain, and will never feel at ease with ourselves. Where there is no coherence or co-operation between what is said and what is done, hypocrisy follows. This automatically creates distance, separation and a lack of trust. When trust is absent, there is no solidarity and no one is willing to come together.

SOME GUIDELINES

To take the first step in achieving real co-operation between the internal and external worlds, it is important to bear these thoughts in mind every day:

1. 'To establish a sense of peace I will look within at my original self' – notice how this core peace puts a full stop to wasteful thoughts and feelings, and keeps us in harmony.
2. 'I spend time in silence. I turn inwards and experience the peace that brings release from selfishness' – remembering

that selfishness damages the co-operation between our inner and outer worlds.

WORKING WITH OTHERS

If a shared task is to be truly successful, it needs to be satisfying to everyone – all those involved need to feel benefit and accomplishment and the honour of having played a part. The most prominent person may be called a leader, but a genuine leader is able to facilitate this appreciative participation and collective feeling of honour.

How do we develop this? Not by expecting or demanding co-operation because we happen to be the leader, teacher or parent. Co-operation is earned through trust; trust facilitates integration and unity. If a selfish person proposes an idea, people will pick up on that selfish motive and be less willing to co-operate. There will be hesitation and doubt. When a task is suggested in a state of selflessness, trust is generated and people are willing to give all of themselves.

Doubts put holes in a task. It is like a bucket containing holes; no matter how much water is poured in, it never gets full and consequently cannot function as a bucket. Think of a task, relationship or goal as the bucket. If we do not plug those holes of doubt, no matter how much motivation, good words and new ideas we pour in, they will drain away.

Doubts are easily plugged through sincerity of intention. When starting something new, we must ask, 'Will everyone benefit or just me? Am I respecting the other people involved or simply using them?' This is especially important when considering relationships. We must always consider whether we are using another person to fill the gaps in our own needs, or whether we are appreciating the other person for what he or she really is. When there is mutual respect, what we offer each other can only be complementary and never parasitical.

CONTEMPLATION

- I sit quietly and look within.
- I concentrate on the thought, 'I am a spiritual being, a soul, a being of peace.'
- I am released from stress and worry.
- With this awareness of deep peace, I understand the value of the eternal principle of non-violence.
- Co-operation follows quite naturally.
- This experience of peace stabilises me and brings unity.

GETTING IT RIGHT

Many people find it difficult to co-operate. If a mother and father do not co-operate and are in conflict, insisting, refusing, not listening, their children are left confused and start to imitate their parents' example. The same is true of governmental cabinets, hospitals and schools – in fact, anywhere that groups of people interact. We need to devote energy over a long period to cultivating awareness of others. This creates a feeling of belonging and makes parasitical relationships less likely – these are relationships in which each person is preoccupied in living off the other, leading to feelings of loneliness, abandonment or rejection.

If you feel fragmented by people and situations, take a little time out to be quiet. Co-operating with silence in this way gives us the peace we need to be able to co-operate with the outside world. By looking inside, we become able to observe the obstacles to co-operation (which often come back to selfishness). When we make the decision to conquer them, the mind feels peaceful and we become able to co-operate with anything and anyone – at any level – without fear or conflict. We become free, at one with ourselves, with God and with the play of life. That is true power.

About the Brahma Kumaris

The Brahma Kumaris is a network of organisations in over 100 countries, with its spiritual headquarters in Mt Abu, India. The University works at all levels of society for positive change.

Acknowledging the intrinsic worth and goodness of the inner self, the University teaches a practical method of meditation that helps people to cultivate their inner strengths and values.

The University also offers courses and seminars in such topics as positive thinking, overcoming anger, stress relief and self-esteem, encouraging spirituality in daily life. This spiritual approach is also brought into healthcare, social work, education, prisons and other community settings.

The University's Academy in Mount Abu, Rajasthan, India, offers individuals from all backgrounds a variety of life-long learning opportunities to help them recognise their inherent qualities and abilities in order to make the most of their lives.

All courses and activities are offered free of charge.

Visit www.brahmakumaris.org for more information.

How and Where to Find Out More

Spiritual Headquarters

PO Box No 2, Mount Abu 307501,
Rajasthan, India
Tel: (+91) 2974-238261 to 68
Fax: (+91) 2974-238883
E-mail: abu@bkivv.org

International Co-Ordinating Office & Regional Office for Europe and the Middle East

Global Co-operation House,
65-69 Pound Lane,
London, NW10 2HH, UK
Tel: (+44) 020-8727-3350
Fax: (+44) 020-8727-3351
E-mail: london@brahmakumaris.org

REGIONAL OFFICES

Africa

Global Museum for a Better World,
Maua Close,
off Parklands Road, Westlands
PO Box 123, Sarit Centre, Nairobi,
Kenya
Tel: (+254) 20-374-3572
Fax: (+254) 20-374-3885
E-mail: nairobi@brahmakumaris.org

Australia and South East Asia

78 Alt Street, Ashfield, Sydney,
NSW 2131, Australia
Tel: (+61) 2-9716-7066
Fax: (+61) 2-9716-7795
E-mail: ashfield@au.brahmakumaris.org

The Americas and the Caribbean

Global Harmony House,
46 S. Middle Neck Road,
Great Neck, NY 11021, USA
Tel: (+1) 516-773-0971
Fax: (+1) 516-773-0976
E-mail: newyork@brahmakumaris.org

Russia, Cis and the Baltic countries

2 Gospitalnaya Ploschad, build. 1,
Moscow 111020, Russia
Tel: (+7) 495-263-0247
Fax: (+7) 495-261-3224
E-mail: moscow@brahmakumaris.org